BOOK OF TREES
MID-ATLANTIC TREES EDITION
Children's Forest and Tree Books

SPEEDY
PUBLISHING

Speedy Publishing LLC
40 E. Main St. #1156
Newark, DE 19711
www.speedypublishing.com

There are
approximately 100,00
known species of
trees in the world.

Magnolia grandiflora is a medium to large evergreen tree which may grow 120 feet tall.

Throughout the spring and summer, the large flowers of the Magnolia grandiflora tree open and release their strong, pleasant fragrance, reminiscent of lemons.

The American chestnut can reach up to 30 metres in height and 3 metres in diameter.

The American Chestnut is valued for its fruit and lumber. The American chestnut was a very important tree for wildlife, providing much of the fall mast for species.

The black
walnut is a large
deciduous tree
attaining heights
of 30-40 meters.

Black walnut
trees often
stand alone
in the forest
because their
roots and dead
leaves produce
juglone, a toxic
chemical that
can kill other
vegetation.

The paperbark maple It is a small to medium-sized deciduous tree, reaching 6-9 meters tall.

Paperback
maple's bark is
smooth, shiny
orange-red,
peeling in thin,
papery layers.

The American plum grows as a large shrub or small tree, reaching up to 15 feet.

American
plum grows
in prairies,
woodlands,
pastures, and
along roadsides
and riverbanks.

The black locust is an invasive species. If the black locust has been introduced to a new environment, it tends to compete with native species and take over in that environment.

Black locust
is used for
fenceposts, mine
timbers, poles,
railroad ties, ship
timbers, wooden
pins, pegs, nails,
stakes, boxes,
crates, pulpwood,
fuelwood, and
novelties.

Redbud tree is small tree. It develops 6 to 10 inches wide trunk that can grow 15 to 30 feet in height.

Redbud tree
has gray or
brownish bark
that is smooth
in young trees.
Redbud tree
produces heart-
shaped leaves
with pointed tips.

 The American elm is an extremely hardy tree that can withstand winter temperatures as low as -42 °C.

A young American elm grows quickly, eventually reaching a height of 80 to 100 feet.

The
serviceberry
can grow to 0.2-
20 m tall; some
are small trees
and some are
multistemmed.

The fruit of
several species
of serviceberry
are excellent to
eat raw. Fruit
is harvested
locally for pies
and jams.

Visit
BABY PROFESSOR
EDUCATION KIDS
www.BabyProfessorBooks.com
to download Free Baby Professor eBooks
and view our catalog of new and exciting
Children's Books